A Proverb A Day

Allen Lyle

Copyright © 2024

All rights reserved.

No part of this publication may be reproduced, distributed, or transmitted in any form or by any means, including photocopying, recording, or other electronic or mechanical methods, without the author's prior written permission, except in the case of brief quotations embodied in critical reviews and certain other non-commercial uses permitted by copyright law. For permission requests, please get in touch with the author.

Contents

Dedication i
Acknowledgments ii
About the Author iii
Preface 1
Proverbs 1 4
Proverbs 2 6
Proverbs 3 9
Proverbs 4 12
Proverbs 5 14
Proverbs 6 16
Proverbs 7 18
Proverbs 8 20
Proverbs 9 22
Proverbs 10 24
Proverbs 11 26
Proverbs 12 29
Proverbs 13 31
Proverbs 14 34
Proverbs 15 36
Proverbs 16 38
Proverbs 17 40
Proverbs 18 42
Proverbs 19 44
Proverbs 20 46
Proverbs 21 48
Proverbs 22 50

Proverbs 23 52
Proverbs 24 54
Proverbs 25 56
Proverbs 26 58
Proverbs 27 60
Proverbs 28 63
Proverbs 29 65
Proverbs 30 68
Proverbs 31 71
Conclusion 73

Dedication

To all those who seek wisdom, knowledge, and understanding from the Father

Acknowledgments

I would like to start by expressing my heartfelt thanks to my brother in Christ, colleague, and accountability partner, Gene Williams for his shared belief in the power of Proverbs. Without his encouragement, support, and willingness to be a sounding board to countless venting sessions, this book would never have seen the light of day.

Additionally, I am eternally grateful to my amazing publishing team who held my hand throughout this journey. To Alan Khan, John Nelson, Roy Harper, Walter Krasniqi, and Zach Francis who made sure all my errors were corrected, designed an amazing book cover, and put some much-needed spit-n-polish on this old country boy. To Daniel Lock who made sure I was on the right track from the get-go and successfully convinced me to trust this project to his team of creative artists. And, finally, to Mike Ramos, my literary Project Manager who acted as a beacon that lit my new path as an author step-by-step.

About the Author

Allen Lyle is an award-winning actor, writer, director, singer, and songwriter. He began acting at the age of 8, portraying Santa Claus in his school Christmas play. Apparently, the acting bug was deeply entrenched within that first "Ho-ho-ho" because he went on to star in numerous stage productions that ranged the gamut from drama to comedy to musicals. Additionally, he has landed roles in both local and national commercials, and he has one SAG movie under his acting belt. In his teens and early 20's, Allen's stage presence combined with his faith, and he began a regular circuit traveling to area churches performing Gospel ventriloquism. In the mid 1990's, he was tapped to be an anchor for the local NBC affiliate Morning News, spending six years in that capacity. From there, Allen co-hosted a national television show for ten years as a home improvement expert, during which time the show was nominated for an Emmy award. In a 20/20 hindsight glance at his life, Allen says he has lived more in a single lifetime than most get to in 3 or 4. In his own words, "I have wrestled a timber wolf, gone roller skating with Bill Nye the Science Guy, flown with the Blue Angels, went deep sea fishing with Hank Aaron, and got kissed by Patti LaBelle, but without hesitation I can tell you that my favorite role has been that of father and grandfather."

Preface

Let me start by stating an obvious fact: I am not a Bible scholar. Yes, I have had many university hours logged in the study of Bible doctrine. Yes, I am a Bible-believing, born again, washed in the blood, marching to Zion, saved by grace, heaven bound when the roll is called up yonder, an unworthy sinner who accepted the gift of God purchased on the old rugged cross. I was raised in the Southern Baptist Convention church, transitioned to independent Baptists, to fundamental Baptists, turned away from the fundamentalists when they started appearing to be more like fanatical holy terrorists, moved to the Christian church organization where I was ordained an elder, and eventually settled into the "beyond the Autumn of my life" years simply happy to enjoy any pastor or evangelist that spoke the true, doctrinal word of God without emphasis on putting my name on their roster.

One of the traits I have long believed in as a Christian is to have a daily time of devotion where you are spending quality, uninterrupted time in prayer, study, and worship to God. I have read countless devotionals and books, including Our Daily Bread, Morning and Evening, along with several books by such authors as D.L. Moody, Charles Spurgeon, Albert Barnes, RC Sproul, Adrian Rodgers, G. Campbell Morgan, and Bruce Wilkinson.

No matter what book or devotional I have used, my personal quiet time ALWAYS included spending time in God's Word, the Bible. Now, if you are a staunch, King James Version-only advocate, well… God bless you. I, personally, don't believe that you can only hear God through a translation from the year 1611. I do use the KJV frequently, but I also enjoy the New International Version, the New Living Translation, the New KJV, the Amplified Bible, the Christian Standard Bible, and a whole host of other notable translations. Additionally, I frequently use my Greek/English Interlinear New Testament, the Septuagint, and I absolutely couldn't get by without my well-worn Strong's Concordance in conjunction with the Moody Press Theological Wordbook of the Old Testament for researching the Hebrew texts.

One of the first suggestions given to me as a young believer was to read one chapter of the book of Proverbs each day for a month since there are 31 chapters in the book. I discovered that no matter how many months I have done this, I tend to learn something new each time I read a daily chapter. Thus, you have the reason for my writing this devotional. I wanted to share my "discoveries" for each day in one particular month. What follows are expounded thoughts based on my reading of the Proverbs in January of 2024. You'll see that my method of diving into the Word of God is through laser-focused, in-depth word studies. I have found that the meanings and choice of the Hebrew language are so much more expressive than our understanding of our Americanized grammar. I will also explore the various translations for a more colloquial expression of the passage.

My hope is that you not only receive a portion of the blessing that God has given me through these thoughts but that you will also take up the challenge to read a chapter of Proverbs a day for just one month and see for yourself what the Lord will reveal to you.

But above all else, take the blessing you receive that day and share it with others.

Proverbs 1

I always read the full chapter out loud. While reading it, one or two verses will typically "jump off the text" and land right in my face. No matter where in the chapter this happens, I continue to read aloud the full text before going back to the ones that left an impression. Today, as I began the Proverbs anew, it was verses 5 and 6 taken from the **New Living Translation**:

> "⁵*Let the wise listen to these proverbs and become even wiser. Let those with understanding receive guidance*
> ⁶ *by exploring the meaning in these proverbs and parables, the words of the wise and their riddles."*

An empty-headed, mindless reading of the Bible will rarely yield fruit. Here, the inspired words of King Solomon tell us that in no uncertain terms should we believe that wisdom, guidance, knowledge, and understanding will be ours without effort on our part. I was keenly focused on the phrase, "*by exploring the meaning*" when reading today's passage.

Have you ever put any thought into what life was like for an explorer in days gone by? My mind goes immediately to the likes of Marco Polo, Vasco da Gama, Ferdinand Magellan, and Sir Walter Raleigh. Early explorers navigated vast, uncharted territories, driven by curiosity and the pursuit of new lands and the possibility of tremendous riches in spices, gold, or jewels. From perilous seas, unknown diseases, and indigenous cultures, they relied on primitive navigation tools and sheer determination. Each voyage was a gamble between discovery, danger, and sometimes death. The life of an explorer was marked by a mix of excitement, uncertainty, and the constant thrill of venturing into the unknown. It was not a career meant for the faint of heart.

The **KJV** translation simply states, *"To understand a proverb…"*, which doesn't quite convey the true meaning unless you "explore" more. The Hebrew text from this verse uses the word, בִּין, (bene), which literally means to separate mentally. Think about an impossible magic trick you've seen. How did he do that?!?! You start to deconstruct the trick in your mind. Reverse engineer it. What sort of misdirection was used? How could a full-grown adult elephant fit inside a 2' x 2' box? Okay, I never saw a trick like that, but if I had, it would've blown my feeble brain to bits.

My takeaway: When it comes to really understanding these proverbs that are about to be shared, you are required to dig in…break a sweat…blaze a trail through an overgrown thicket until your muscles ache. How can I possibly understand a proverb? By exploring the meaning! Mentally separate it into bite-sized morsels. Break out the reference books and conduct word studies. Log onto the Internet and search through commentaries. Get more than one Bible translation in front of you and read the passage in all translations, and study (explore) thoroughly.

Proverbs 2

Yesterday, we launched into the book of Proverbs with a chapter dedicated to the beginning of wisdom. Today's chapter focuses on the value of that wisdom. What spoke to me today was the kickoff with an "If – Then" passage. In the 5th verse we read the following taken from the **New King James Version**:

> "*5 Then you will understand the fear of the Lord,*
> *And find the knowledge of God.*"

However, it was the "If" verses that piqued my interest. Verse 5 is what our goal should be. Verses 1-4 tell us how to get there. Here is a plain step-by-step as read in the **New Living Translation**:

> "*1 My child, listen to what I say,*
> *and treasure my commands.*
> *2 Tune your ears to wisdom,*
> *and concentrate on understanding.*
> *3 Cry out for insight,*
> *and ask for understanding.*
> *4 Search for them as you would for silver;*
> *seek them like hidden treasures.*"

1. *Listen* – From the Hebrew לָקַח (law-kakh') to take or accept. It will be neither carelessly nor conveniently dropped into your lap. You have to reach out and take it.

2. *Treasure* – From the Hebrew צָפַן (tsaw-fan') to hide by covering over. The same word is used to describe Moses' mother when she hid him in the bullrushes. It is hiding away a priceless treasure.

3. *Tune* – From the Hebrew קָשַׁב (kaw-shab') to prick up the ears. This is a unique word found only here. It is typically used when describing animals when they hear something that promotes caution or concern. At that instance, when their ears prick up, nothing else matters, and full attention is placed on listening intently!

4. *Concentrate* – From the Hebrew נָטָה (naw-taw') to stretch or spread out. Think of a great elastic material, possibly that of a trampoline. You stretch it to the max, covering your understanding of God's Word. And, like such a fabric, onslaughts from without will strike the material (your concentration) and be deflected.

5. *Cry out/Ask* – These are two separate words. The first, קָרָא (kaw-raw') denotes calling out by name. The insight you need can only come from God. Others will offer false insight, so cry out to him by name. The second word, נָתַן (naw-than'), means to give or pour out. It's not a matter of asking a simple, "Hey, God, can I have some understanding?" It's pouring out your heart and soul, pleading for Him to give you an understanding of His Word.

6. *Search/Seek* – I find it interesting that the **NLT** reverses the order of these words as written in the **King James Version**. The Hebrew translated in the **NLT** as "search" בָּקַשׁ (baw-kash') means to strive after through worship or prayer, while the word translated as "seek" חָפַשׂ (khaw-fas') means to make a diligent search, with the emphasis on the diligence more than the search.

My takeaway: If God grants my request for wisdom, knowledge, and understanding, then I need to understand just how valuable it is. And, when seeking to be led by His Spirit, then all my attention should be focused on hearing that still, small voice.

Proverbs 3

There will be another 28 chapters worth of proverbs as we continue through the month, but like any decent manual, it all starts with the proper directions. We've seen the beginning of wisdom in chapter 1 and the value of wisdom in chapter 2. Today, in chapter 3, we will be instructed on what to do with this newfound wisdom as we receive it.

The verses that spoke to me are 1-3. Here is the scripture as seen in the **New King James Version**:

> *"¹ My son, do not forget my law,*
> *But let your heart keep my commands;*
>
> *² For length of days and long life*
> *And peace they will add to you.*
>
> *³ Let not mercy and truth forsake you;*
> *Bind them around your neck,*
> *Write them on the tablet of your heart."*

When Solomon says to "keep" these commandments, he uses the word, נָצַר (*naw-tsar'*), which means to guard, protect, and maintain. It's not enough to just be familiar with the proverbs being shared. We must protect these priceless treasures. Gathering and marinating on these pearls of wisdom will result in a happy, peaceful existence even when we are surrounded by war, strife, conflict, and chaos.

We're told to "bind" these proverbs around our neck. This refers to a tradition of literally physically printing out the commands and tying them on a cord and wearing it as a necklace. Some would make them into headbands and tie them to their foreheads. The illustration is that no matter where you go, the commands (proverbs) will always be with you in a real and physical sense. Now, this isn't something you are required to actually do, although it's not a bad idea. I keep a chain that has a shield on the end of it with the traits of the "full armor of God" printed on it. It serves as a reminder to me that I am geared up and prepared for anything Satan may throw my way.

However, to ensure we do "keep" these proverbs, we are instructed to write them on the "tablet" of our hearts. This is a figurative use of the words, so don't rush out in search of an open-heart surgeon who performs a tattoo service on the side. I do find it interesting, though, that it's not recommended we merely memorize these proverbs to the best of our ability, but when you read of the precise location we are commanded.... the TABLET of our heart...well, THIS is a pure theological jewel here. The word לוּחַ (*loo'-akh*) refers to a board or plank that was used instead of using papyrus or stone. Because wood planks would quickly degrade due to the climate, in order to preserve a wood document longer, the plank would be finely and meticulously polished. Interestingly enough, the primary root meaning of *loo'-akh* is to glisten or be polished. In other words, these proverbs aren't just hastily scribbled on the outer surface of my heart (figuratively speaking), but they are inscribed, etched, tattooed…. on the innermost "polished" portion of my heart. The **NLT** says it more succinctly when it states that you should write these golden nuggets of wisdom *"deep within your heart."*

My takeaway: The Holy Scriptures are a gift from God – inspired words by the Father written by faithful followers. There are times I won't have a physical copy of the Bible, but if I take the time and effort to commit as many verses as possible to memory, it will always be with me.

Proverbs 4

This is such a wonderful chapter. Here, we see a loving father dishing out sage advice meant to benefit his children, as long as they pay attention and don't ignore his advice. I absolutely love the admonishment given in verse 25, seen here from the **NLT**:

*"²⁵ Look straight ahead,
and fix your eyes on what lies before you."*

It reminds me of the countless times I've heard a teacher announce to the class during a test, *"Keep your eyes on your own paper! Don't look at your neighbor's test to copy answers!"*

However, there's an even greater reason to keep your eyes forward. Have you ever been driving a car and, for any odd reason, turned your head to the left or right, possibly in an attempt to grab an item from the seat or floor, only to discover the car started veering out of its lane in the same direction you are looking or leaning? That's a potential disaster in the making! A safe driver is one who keeps their eyes on the road or as our passage states, on *"what lies before you."*

My thoughts also turn to the time when the Israelites were wandering in the desert prior to their entry to the land promised to them (**Numbers 21**). God sent poisonous snakes when the Israelites began to complain, of all things, about how they didn't like the food they were eating. Many Israelites died as a result. Upon confession of their sin, they pleaded for Moses to ask God to take away the snakes. Instead, God instructed Moses to fabricate a snake from bronze and put it up on a pole. From then on, anyone bitten by a snake just had to *"fix their eyes"* on the bronze snake, and they wouldn't die. Look anywhere else, and they'd likely be taking a dirt nap.

The proverbs we see in this amazing Old Testament book can give us so much joy, but we need to keep our eyes front, not sideways. One of the mantras I try to live by is "Onward and Upward." Progress isn't just <u>ANY</u> movement. Progress is <u>FORWARD</u> movement. Progress is <u>UPWARD</u> movement. In order to keep that progress flowing, we have to fix our eyes on the Christ of the cross. Take your eyes off Him, and we start to drift to the left or the right. Lateral movement does nothing but remove you from the path you should be on. It sends you careening into the ditch or into a head-on collision.

My takeaway: The devil will do everything he can think of to distract you. He doesn't just want your soul when you die; he wants your eyes while you live. Ignore him! *"Look straight ahead and fix your eyes on what lies before you."* Look to Jesus!

Proverbs 5

There may be some who think they can just skip Chapter 5. You see, this particular chapter deals with the pitfalls of becoming involved with an immoral woman. You may say, "Well, this certainly doesn't apply to me. I can't possibly learn any valuable life lesson from this chapter of Proverbs."

Before you jump ship, let me emphasize that "*ALL* scripture is profitable…" This is also a great example of how reading passages from various translations can help open your eyes to a valuable lesson. The second half of verse 12 is what planted its flag on my turf today. The gist of what's going on leading up to verse 12 is Solomon describing the evils of an immoral woman and how, even though there is a moment of temporary pleasure and ecstasy, the end result is bitterness and misery. Afterwards, it has you reprimanding yourself. If you read the **KJV**, it reads like this:

"12 How I have hated instruction and my heart despised reproof."

The **NLT**, however, puts this in a current vernacular, and it definitely resonates a mighty truth:

"12 If only I had not ignored all the warnings!"

This simple statement reminds me that I cannot plead ignorance of the law. It very plainly says "*all*" the warnings…..Plural….. What makes God's grace so amazing is how many times He allows you opportunities to do the right thing before dropping the hammer on you. Yet, in hindsight, there have been MULTIPLE warnings and red flags that I should have heeded. But, even in my failure, I can find comfort in how my future steps are directed.

Realizing the weight of ignored warnings is a crucial pivoting point in our Christian journey. It's not about dwelling on regret but harnessing its power. Each misstep is a lesson, a beacon guiding toward wiser choices. Embrace the knowledge gained; it's the foundation of growth. Shift the narrative from "*if only*" to "*from now on.*" Use this insight as fuel for future decisions, relying on God's Holy Spirit to steer us toward the preferred path of righteousness.

My takeaway: Acknowledging the past empowers us to shape a better tomorrow by submitting our will to that of God. Remember, every setback is a chance to soar higher, armed with the wisdom of hindsight.

Proverbs 6

There's so much to choose from in this chapter! I could focus on the analogy of looking at the industrious nature of the ant. It would be a good jumping off point, but this month, what stood out to me was the dire warning we need to consider as we make our choices in life. Verses 12 – 15 describe the evil, wicked person. While it's true the description given conjures up a caricature of Snidely Whiplash from the Dudley Do-Right cartoons, it's a broad description that could very well pertain to every one of us. I have a friend who likes to put it this way: *"We're all just one bad decision away from being a lying, thieving, adulterous murderer."* (Credit goes to Gene Williams)

It's a fact that we serve, worship, and praise a gracious and merciful God full of grace. But we should realize….no, scratch that…. We absolutely MUST be aware that a continued walk down a wicked road WILL come to a sudden end, typically when we least expect it.

The **KJV** states this in the latter half of verse 15:

"*15…suddenly shall he be broken without remedy.*"

The **New Living Translation** puts it more bluntly:

"*15 … broken in an instant with no hope of healing.*"

Let's face it. Today's Christians have been spoiled by the patience of a loving and merciful God. Grace has been defined as unmerited favor. You need to put the emphasis on unmerited because if any of us continues making poor (evil) choices, the end of grace won't be a matter of IF, but WHEN. There will be consequences. As Christians, we won't suffer the fate of the non-believer of which this passage is speaking, but we can still learn from it.

The term "broken" translated from the Hebrew יִשָּׁבֵר (shaw-bar'), means to break in pieces… to shatter. If you break a piece off of a vase, superglue does wonders. But if the vase is shattered… it gets tossed into the garbage. This is highlighted in the word for remedy and the description in the **NLT** version. מַרְפֵּא (mar-pay') means a cure, but when used in the negative sense, as we see here, then it means there is "no hope" of a cure. None. At that point in time, the line separating grace from merited favor has been crossed.

My takeaway: Even though I am an adopted child of God, my continued sin will eventually result in being broken and shattered. Until I confess and repent, I may find myself a recipient of God's justice and not His mercy.

Proverbs 7

One of the recurring themes you'll find in Proverbs is the warning against the immoral or promiscuous woman. However, I would also remind you that even if a particular singled-out sin is the topic, you can apply the lesson across the broad field of living the Christian life. Today, a single phrase jumped out at me. I have looked through over a dozen translations, and they all say virtually the same thing. Here is the **New International Version** translation of the phrase found in verse 22:

"²²...*like an ox going to the slaughter.*"

Throughout all the translations, it is written "as" an ox or "like" an ox. Not once does it say "the same as" an ox. Here's the difference. An ox (or substitute any bred-for-food livestock) has no clue that it's about to be killed and made into a backyard BBQ. The foolish young man, or in the broader sense, any human being on the planet, has been given the knowledge that willingly surrendering yourself over to the temporary satisfaction of sin will eventually result in a horrible ending.

It shames me to think of the countless times I've faced temptation of any sort and thought to myself, "Well, maybe just this once" or "I can always ask for forgiveness later." This is why, in my opinion, the term "fool" is given to the young man. Only an idiot (I'm looking in the mirror) would willingly surrender to a sin that can lead nowhere but to destruction. If that ox had even the vaguest amount of intelligence and knew he was about to be the headliner at

Ruth's Chris, he would do an about-face and trample over anyone who stood in his way to run in the opposite direction.

My takeaway: I'll be the first to admit that I'm not the sharpest tool in the shed, but I do know that I've been given the common sense to know right from wrong. Today, I choose to NOT be like an ox, to NOT be labeled a fool, to NOT allow the flattering lips of ANY sin to lead me down the path to destruction.

Proverbs 8

What an amazing and stark contrast this chapter is to the one we read yesterday! In chapter 7, Solomon warned of the wicked and evil wiles of immorality and adultery. The woman pictured was calling out to all "in the black and dark night." She is skulking around in the shadows, walking the streets, standing on the corner near her house. It conjures visions of a spider sitting on her web just waiting for a morsel of man to destroy and consume.

Come the morning, and chapter 8, our attention is directed toward another woman. Not one creeping around at night, whispering sweet nothings…. oh, no, not at all. Today we see Wisdom calling out to the very same people. No whispering either. She "calls out" and she "raises her voice" as is aptly described in the **NLT**:

"*¹ Listen as Wisdom calls out!*
Hear as understanding raises her voice!
² On the hilltop along the road,
she takes her stand at the crossroads.
³ By the gates at the entrance to the town,
on the road leading in, she cries aloud."

Notice how the personification of Wisdom doesn't rely on darkness or secrecy. Pay close attention to where you find her calling out:

"On the hilltop"

"At the crossroads"

"By the gates that enter the city"

"On the road leading in"

The **Septuagint** says she "sings" her words. This is a touring concert you can't help but notice! To me it paints a picture of a town crier roaming the city, calling out to everyone to hear. It could be a warning, or an important edict, or perhaps vital instructions about an approaching event. To willfully turn your back and ignore the message is lunacy.

Once again, we have a strong case supporting the whole "ignorance of the law is no excuse" scenario. Wisdom is making it a point to be wherever it needs to be in order to be heard. The only way on God's green earth you cannot hear the message is by stubbornly plugging up your ears while shouting, "LA-LA-LA-LA-LA-LA-LA-LA-LA!" in an attempt to drown out the message.

My takeaway: Hear me out. There's not an actual angelic being called Wisdom outside caterwauling for our educational edification, but there are Christian brothers and sisters, pastors, evangelists, multiple books, devotionals, and above all, the written Word of God where we can find wisdom any day, any hour, any place. Both Wisdom and Sin are courting us. It's all on us, though, to decide which one we're going to go steady with.

Proverbs 9

Today, I am drawn to the 6th verse of this chapter. The **New International Version** states:

"*⁶ Leave your simple ways and you will live;"*

But the **King James Version** puts it more plainly:

"*⁶ Forsake the foolish and live;"*

Lest you think this is a recipe for long life, let's break down the key words here. When you "leave" or "forsake" anything, it means to completely turn your back on it and don't look back. What are you forsaking? The Hebrew word translated as "foolish" in the **KJV** and "simple" in the **NIV** is פְּתִי (peth-ee') which means naïve or immature. But this word is also descriptive of one who is seducible. Seduction can come from many sources. We tend to think of seduction as only associated with sexual morality (or as is often the case, immorality), but we can also be seduced by money, power, fame, and possessions. Turning your back on any seduction is hard to do, but we have been given a superlative motivation. Do so and live.

The Hebrew word is חָיָה (khaw-yaw'). The connotation of this word is that you are made alive, quickened, but not as if you were born and – poof! – you're alive. This word pertains to being revived from a sickness. Living foolishly is, indeed, a sickness. Our health, our longevity, our redeeming grace come from listening to the Word of God and completely turning our backs on the seduction of whatever the world is throwing at us in an attempt to keep us sick, dying, and bedridden. This "khaw-yaw" not only revives us, but it also sustains us, or as some translations convey, it allows us to continue or remain alive.

My takeaway: Today, I choose to forsake the seduction of the world. Today, I choose the antidote for my sickness. Today, I choose to live. Today, I choose God.

Proverbs 10

Up until today, we've read chapters that have an overall theme or two. As we begin chapter 10, we get into the "heart" of Solomon's proverbs. Each verse becomes its own thought, and the nuggets of wisdom pour out like a steady rainfall. It becomes almost difficult to choose just one thought, but let's move forward in the attempt!

With so many wonderful verses, I was almost shocked that the one I focused on today was in verse 16. Here it is in the **King James Version:**

> *"16 The labour of the righteous tendeth to life: the fruit of the wicked to sin."*

My first thought was to break down some key words. It was the first half of the verse that touched me, so let's look at the words, labour, righteous, and tendeth.

Labour: פעלה (peh-oo-law') – recompense or reward for work accomplished

Righteous: צדיק (tsad-deek') – to be just, or to be made right.

Tendeth: um……... where's the Hebrew? Hello? ....

Well, this is embarrassing. My Hebrew reference tells me there is no word here. In fact, this was an added portion of the translation by the **King James** team of translators. A better translation, in my opinion, is found in the **NIV** or the **NLT**:

> *"16 The wages of the righteous is life."* **NIV**

> *"16 The earnings of the godly enhance their lives."* **NLT**

My takeaway: Paul, in the book of Romans, tells us that *"There is none righteous. No, not one."* I can rejoice, though, because as the Hebrew translation tells me, I can be MADE right. It's true that all my righteousness is as *"filthy rags,"* but because God looks at me through the saving blood of Christ, He sees a robe of pure white. The things I do in this life, my work, and my wage for that work should always lean toward doing right though the help and power of the Holy Spirit. Through the effort and sweat equity of this work, I will be rewarded with life, and life eternal.

Proverbs 11

With so many wonderful pearls to find in this chapter, I was a little confused as to why my eyes kept coming back to this particular verse as read in the **NKJV**:

> *"¹² He who is devoid of wisdom despises his neighbor, but a man of understanding holds his peace."*

Being obedient to the Holy Spirit's leading, I jumped right into the deep end and discovered something extremely vital for those who are walking in Christ.

Our first word study goes to חָסֵר (khaw-sare'). Here, it is translated as "devoid." It refers to a complete lack of or being destitute. It is the very same word used in the negative sense in Exodus when it relates to the story of the Israelites being fed manna in the wilderness. Because of God's grace, they never lacked for nourishment. In our text today, it describes an individual with a complete lack of wisdom.

But the real prize of this verse comes in the word given as "neighbor." The Hebrew word is רֵעַ (ray'-ah). It does not necessarily mean the guy living right next door to your house. In fact, the word is most commonly used to represent a friend, a companion… someone with whom you have either a close or a familiar relationship. It can be a brother, sister, spouse, or any family member. Do not confuse this verse to be applicable to an enemy. The Bible very clearly identifies the difference. In fact, the word "enemy" and its spelling variations are found 276 times in the Scriptures.

Yes, we are instructed to love our enemies. To pray for those who despitefully use us. This 12th verse of Proverbs 11 is not about how we treat our enemies. It's how we are instructed to treat our friends, loved ones, colleagues. There's an old saying that goes like this: "You always hurt the ones you love." This should never, never, ever be the case with a child of God.

I tend to believe that this was the very verse Jesus was thinking of when he instructed his disciples to "love one another." It could also have been the verse in His mind when being tested by the Pharisees as we read in Matthew 22:34-40. Jesus recites the two greatest commandments of "the Law and the Prophets" and said, "Love your neighbor as yourself."

In Proverbs, Solomon paints a clear picture of those who disrespect, abuse, quarrel, and "despise" those who are closest to them. That picture is a Polaroid of those with a complete lack of common sense. Jesus reminds us that His commandment (not suggestion) is to show them love. And, if we have a difficult time doing so, "hold our peace." That's a tactful way of saying keep your big mouth shut. In fact, the Hebrew word for "holds his peace" is actually a single word: חָרַשׁ (khaw-rash'). In this context, it means "to be deaf in accompaniment to being mute."

My takeaway: Quit stirring up the pot! Treat your friends, family, and your inner circle with the same respect you want from them.

John 15:12 records this statement made by Jesus. It is the penultimate in commandments and relates 100% to today's proverb:

"This is My commandment, that you love one another as I have loved you."

Proverbs 12

As I was reading today's chapter, verse 23 jumped out like a theological jack-in-the-box. We'll start with the **NLT**:

"²³ The wise don't make a show of their knowledge, but fools broadcast their foolishness."

At first glance, this may appear to be a bit contradictory from what we were taught in the very first chapter. We should be seeking out knowledge, wisdom, and understanding. Now you're telling me if I obtain this goal, not to display it?

Actually, a more understandable explanation would be to use the vernacular, "Nobody likes a show-off."

Our focus is on two actions: Make a show of and Broadcast.

Now, as someone whose background has been steeped in both theatre and television, I tend to always WANT to make a show or broadcast. Let's dive deeper into these words and phrases.

Make A Show

The **KJV** uses the single verb, "conceal." The literal translation of the Hebrew word used, כָּסָה (kaw-saw') means to cover. It's the same word that describes how the frogs covered the land in Egypt during the plagues sent by God to convince Pharaoh to let the Israelites go. In our text, it conveys the idea of camouflage. In other words, we are to diligently seek and ask for wisdom, understanding, and knowledge but not flaunt it as a superiority over others. The reason God reveals knowledge, in my opinion, is for us to be able to share it with others.

Broadcast

Here, the **KJV** goes in the opposite direction using the verb "proclaim." When we dig into the Hebrew writing, the word קָרָא (kaw-raw') is used. Does anyone else find the humor in how very similar those two words are, yet completely opposite? The word means to call out or to name. In some instances, it also suggests the idea of accosting someone you met. It stirs up images of those ridiculous, pompous "wrestlers" you see on TV bragging about themselves and can only speak in a decibel level equal to that of a freight train. They quite literally broadcast their foolishness.

My takeaway: As we go through today, let's continue to seek wisdom and knowledge that we can quietly and reverently share with others. Conceal any appearance of being a peacock, lording our wisdom over others.

Proverbs 13

It was early 20th-century writer and art critic James Huneker who said, "All men of action are dreamers." Quite often, in my vast and varied career, I have been called a dreamer. Oddly, though, when the term has been used to describe me, it has never been in a positive light. It was said to me in a chastising manner. It's as though being a dreamer was looked down upon... scorned... ridiculed.

Personally, I enjoy being a dreamer. It fuels my imagination and, at times, gives me a somewhat lofty goal to attain. Today's devotional and quiet time seemed to give me some vindication.

There were two verses that spoke to me today. Let's begin with verse 12, then jump to verse 19, both from the **NLT**:

> "*12 Hope deferred makes the heart sick,*
> *but a dream fulfilled is a tree of life."*
>
> "*19 It is pleasant to see dreams come true,*
> *but fools refuse to turn from evil to attain them."*

"*A dream fulfilled is a tree of life*" and "*It is pleasant to see dreams come true.*" Both statements, at least for me, tell me that not only is it not such a bad thing to be a dreamer, but there are going to be times when you can expect to see dreams become reality. I think the translation of the **New International Version** pinpoints it better by substituting the word "longing" in the place of "dream."

The Hebrew word, חָמַד (khaw-mad') denotes something so precious, so desired, something that could be easily coveted, or something that provides an intense delight. Now, granted, this could be something good or something evil. There are no redeeming qualities in an intense longing for evil, but is it right for me to have an intense longing for things that are not evil?

In Psalm 19:7-10 we have a laundry list of good things to long for:

1. The law of the Lord
2. The testimony of the Lord
3. The statutes of the Lord
4. The commandment of the Lord
5. The fear of the Lord
6. The judgements of the Lord

All of these are to be more "desired" than gold. The very same word, khaw-mad, is used.

Proverbs 21:20 says (**NKJV**), *"There is desirable treasure, and oil in the dwelling of the wise."* Once again, khaw-mad is used (desirable) to describe what is in the house (dwelling) of the wise. Notice what is mentioned: treasure and oil. Oil was a necessity. It was used along with flour to make food. Oil was needed for lamps to light the way in darkness. But treasure? That wasn't a need. Treasures are wants.... desires.... longings...yes, they are dreams. And where can you expect to find them? In the house of the wise.

My takeaway: If you have a dream or desire, and you can positively prove to yourself that there is no connection to evil; nor could it become an object of worship, then these dreams could very well receive God's stamp of approval. They may even come true.

Proverbs 14

Back in the mid-1970s, Motown founder and legend Berry Gordy decided he wanted to widen his portfolio, so he directed a motion picture called Mahogany. As movies go, I found it to be mediocre. Originally intended as a vehicle for Liza Minelli, it was eventually offered to Diana Ross. The theme song from the movie started out with these lyrics:

Do you know where you're going to?

Do you like the things that life is showing you?

Where are you going to?

Do you know?

These lyrics popped into my mind immediately as I read through today's chapter. My "Name That Tune" moment came in verse 8, **NLT**:

"⁸ The prudent understand where they are going."

Let's go ahead and break this down. First, who are the prudent? The word used is עֲרוּמִים, which is the plural of עָרוּם (aw-room'), meaning one who is crafty, shrewd, sensible. While it appears to be used more often in the negative sense, this is a time it is used as a positive description. I like the **Christian Standard Bible** description: *"The sensible person."*

We've seen this next word before. "Understand", בִּין (bene), a primary root word that means "to discern." This isn't a mere, "Oh, yeah…. I get it" kind of understanding. Merriam-Webster defines discern as *"a verb that means to detect with the eyes, senses, or mind, or to recognize or identify something as separate and distinct."* In other words, time, energy, and effort have been utilized to confirm the validity of a thing. I don't just have a general idea of the direction I'm going, but I know the place, the description, the beauty, the importance, and the reason why I am on this directional path.

דֶּרֶךְ (deh'rek) – *"WHERE they are going."* The Hebrew word means way, road… but in the figurative sense. It more properly can be translated as the journey itself, or the manner in which you make that journey.

My takeaway: As a sensible being and one who seeks the wisdom and understanding that God can provide, I need to make sure that I take the time to fully discern the knowledge given to me. There should be no question or doubt that I have made an intelligent decision based on that knowledge to take the path leading to a richer and fuller relationship with the one, true, Holy God, Creator of all things.

Proverbs 15

A recurring construct in the book of Proverbs is the comparison, e.g., Not this, but that… That, but not this… etc. Today's stand-out verse follows this recipe. In verse 8, we read this, as translated by the **KJV**:

"8 The sacrifice of the wicked is an abomination to the Lord: but the prayer of the upright is his delight."

It's the second half of this verse that stood out to me today, although in order to fully understand it, we need to keep the first half in mind.

Prayer is talking to God. It is a conversation. It is fellowship. It is one of the key foundations to a healthy relationship. This particular word, however, is more along the lines of supplication or to intreat. תְּפִלָּה (tef-il-law") speaks specifically to a prayer of supplication, of asking. This makes perfect sense when compared to the first part of the verse referencing the sacrifice made by the wicked. Yes, we need to have praise for God. We need to offer thanks to God. But we also need to realize that God also takes great delight in having us share our needs with Him in petitioned prayer.

The word "delight" I just referenced comes from the Hebrew word that means desire. Having us call upon God and offering prayers of supplication is something He desires to hear. The root word describes the acceptance of a gift or sacrifice. Again, this is where we see the comparison to the sacrifice given by the wicked.

Something that goes along with this (and I've used this illustration before, so I always caution that I am not meaning to be irreverent), we must not approach God as some cosmic Santa Claus. Yes, He delights.... DESIRES... our supplications, but it is the character of the supplicant that matters. God delights in the prayers of the UPRIGHT.

יָשָׁר (yaw-shawr') means to be straight or even. It pertains to the quality of the heart and mind. This same word is also used to describe an attribute of God Himself. As a carpenter and woodworker, when I see the term "even," I link that with one of my most important tools: my level. I find the "even" status when the level bubble is centered perfectly between two lines. The same applies when I'm looking for an object to be "plumb," which is the same as "upright." Scriptures tell us that all of our righteousness is as filthy rags, yet through the sacrificial blood of Christ, we can be upright.... even.... level.... plumb... by seeking to be like Jesus. That's a difficult thing to accomplish, but it's a great thing to ask for. God delights in that prayer.

My takeaway: Find your balance (even, level, plumb) by asking your heavenly Father for it.

Proverbs 16

I was very pleasantly surprised by the verse that stood out to me today. First of all, because in the many times I have read the Proverbs, this verse seems to have eluded me until today.

Second, it isn't your typical verse that you would think about as something you would hear from today's pulpit.

And third, it helps emphasize my suggestion to read from varying translations. I'm going to start with the **KJV**:

"26 He that laboureth laboureth for himself; for his mouth craveth it of him."

What?!?!? To all my "bless-your-heart" **KJV**-only brothers and sisters: Seriously? *For his mouth craveth it of him*? Even the staunchest KJ-Vite has to admit that this could be stated a little more clearly in today's vernacular without losing its inspiration. Let's move to the **New Living Translation**:

"26 It is good for workers to have an appetite; an empty stomach drives them on."

Even better, the **Berean Study Bible**:

"26 A worker's appetite works for him because his hunger drives him forward."

This does not mean if your stomach is growling, then finish up your project, and you can eat lunch. However, that incentive was used on me many times back in the day when I was building cabinets for my father's construction company.

Quick break down:

The worker (עָמֵל): One who labors, toils, often with or in sorrow.

Appetite (נֶפֶשׁ): Desire, passion, life, soul, emotion

Hunger (פִּיהוּ:): Completely different word than appetite. This 3rd person, masculine noun has a literal translation of "his mouth," but in this context, it can also be translated as his portion or his "according to." That may not make sense but think about it. What is your "according to?" It's your belief. Your core. Your mantra.

Drives (אָכַף): To press or to urge.

Onward (עָלָיו): Defined as above, over, upon. Dare I say it? Onward and upward!

My takeaway: No matter what I am doing, whatever work has me toiling, even in sorrow, the very core of my being, my passion, my desire placed in my heart and soul by the Holy God of Creation should move me ever onward and upward with urgency. As the **NLT** states, it's good for me!

Proverbs 17

A lesson that many people, me included, wish they could have learned at a much younger age is when to keep your mouth shut. I could have easily been the poster child for Foot-in-Mouth Disease.

That brings me to today's verse. It's one that often stands out to me, and this month it did once more. Here is verse 28 as written in the **NKJV**:

"²⁸ Even a fool is counted wise when he holds his peace; When he shuts his lips, he is considered perceptive."

This verse has a parallel with our devotional from Chapter 11, but where our "peace holder" from that chapter was already a true "man of understanding," the tight-lipped fellow in today's verse is a foolish man. It's about appearances. It also provides an excellent example of how following God's advice, even for the foolish, the wicked, and the non-believer… can be beneficial to them.

A full Southern paraphrasing of our verse would sound like this: "Even a knuckleheaded simpleton can fool others to think he's a pretty smart fellow if he keeps his mouth shut. Sure, he may still be a perverse so-and-so, but he can hide it as long as he keeps quiet."

Sadly, most foolish people can't keep quiet for long. It's a tough thing to do! The very word used to describe shutting his lips comes from a Hebrew word אטם (aw-tam') that means to close or shut as a window against its jamb. Now, the jamb is the side portion, which means this would be similar to a casement window. If you only pull it to the jamb, it can be blown right open again. You have to pull it in, hold it tight, then lock it. So, it pays for a foolish person to keep his peace.

However, while this is to his benefit, it is only a mask. It is a fool concealing his folly.

My takeaway: Examine my heart and my motives. Actively seek wisdom, knowledge and understanding. Know the difference between keeping my peace and concealing my folly.

Proverbs 18

I think today's devotional can be seen from two perspectives. First, the perspective of the Receiver. Let's take a look at the verse. This is verse 8, as read in the **NLT**:

"⁸ Rumors are dainty morsels that sink deep into one's heart."

I really liked the wording and was considering several avenues to take this discussion, but then I started digging into the Hebrew texts and discovered the **NLT** is (in my opinion) a little askew on this one. My trusty **King James** reads:

"⁸ The words of a talebearer are as wounds, and they go down into the innermost parts of the belly."

A much better translation, but we still need to dig deeper. Let's begin with the talebearer. Many translations use the word "gossip," while others use "whisperer."

The Hebrew is נִרְגָּן (neer-gawn'), translated as a slanderer. More specifically, one who murmurs. Either way, you're looking at someone who isn't saying anything nice or flattering.

Now, how in the world the **NLT** has "dainty morsels" where the **KJV** says "wounds" is a mystery. I think the **KJV** translators were trying to tie the hurtful words to the next half about the belly, but the literal translation of the Hebrew לָהַם (law-ham') is "bits greedily swallowed."

Ever get invited to a party where "food" is served only to find out it's finger food or a mini slice of cheese on a Ritz cracker? If you're like me and have a tendency to get hangry, you loudly inform the host that you can have Papa John's deliver a meat lover's extra-large within 30 minutes or so to make up for his or her negligence. You can bet dollars to doughnuts that I'm going to clear out an entire platter of pigs-in-a-blanket. That's the picture of "bits greedily swallowed."

I mentioned at the start about two perspectives, so here's #2. Be honest with yourself. Have you, like me, been both the Receiver AND the Deliverer of those rumors? The slander? The "bits" that people will grab and swallow quickly? I'm ashamed of the times I've allowed such hatred to pass through my lips.

And where do those words wind up? In the innermost portions of the people swallowing those words. That includes not just who I've slandered but everyone who heard it and took it to heart as Gospel truth. Shame on me… I've just tossed one of the most important commandments down the tubes: "Love one another just as I have loved you."

My takeaway: My walk and my talk are equally important. My goal as a Christian friend, family member, and even a first-time acquaintance should be to exude the behavior of Jesus, build up those around me, and present myself as a representative of the Kingdom of God. I can't do that with rumors and slander pouring out of my mouth.

Proverbs 19

If you've ever had an individual call you out on some comment you made or action you took, knowing full well that it was wrong, then you'll understand how I'm feeling today after going through Proverbs 19. The verse that jumped out at me was #3. I think the **NLT** puts it very plainly:

> "*³ People ruin their lives by their own foolishness and then are angry at the Lord.*"

Isn't that typical of a conceited individual to want to blame someone else for his own stupidity? It was like being forced to look into a mirror. "*Thou art the man!*" as Samuel put it to King Saul.

A lesser-known translation, The **Names of God Bible**, really puts the kick in the mule:

> "*³ The stupidity of a person turns his life upside down, and his heart rages at Yahweh.*"

There's really not a lot of word study needed here. This is "The Bible for Dummies" explanation. If this were algebra, it would be as follows: $a + b = c$, where a = the foolish thoughts, words or actions of an individual… b = their subsequent blaming God for their troubles resulting from their foolishness… and c = "Here's your sign, stupid!"

The translations above of "*ruin their lives*" and "*turns his life upside down*" comes from the Hebrew סָלַף (saw-laf') that means to twist or distort. It's like so many other avenues touched by the sin of man. What was meant to be good and perfect has been distorted… twisted. A life meant to serve God crumpled up like a dirty tissue after blowing your nose.

Then, we have the audacity to blame our problems on God. Our act of stupidity makes our hearts rage. An interesting comparison comes in the book of Jonah where the very same word translated as "angry" זָעַף (zaw-af') is used to describe the raging sea that Jonah was tossed into just before being swallowed by the whale.

I've been this person. I have blamed God for not being there to answer my every whim, wish, desire, gimme-gimme-gimme list.… It takes a lot of humbling and, often, chastisement by the Holy Spirit to bring you to the realization that the trouble all started with "the stupidity of Allen."

My takeaway: Ask for wisdom… for knowledge… for understanding… and for a well-lit path illuminated by the Holy Spirit. While some trials and troubles may be the result of others, it is all too often due to my own ignorance and refusal to listen to God. Stop being stupid, Allen.

Proverbs 20

As we dig into today's reading, I am going to offer two possible interpretations, both of which, in my opinion, are valid and worthy of consideration. Our verse comes near the end of this chapter. Here is verse 27 in the **KJV**:

"27 The spirit of man is the candle of the Lord, searching all the inward parts of the belly."

Interpretation #1:

Without taking the full context into consideration, this could be confusing. How is it that man's spirit is what God relies on as His "candle" or (using the literal meaning of the Hebrew) His light? I think if this is where someone's confusion comes into play, it's because they are not considering the actual meaning of the spirit of man. For the secularist, this is what Dr. Freud would call a part of the superego, or the conscience. It is our inward Jiminy Cricket that puts a guilt trip on us when we do something that we innately know is wrong.

For the Christian, though, we understand that our inner voice… our "spirit" … is usually a leading, an urging, a compelling of God's Holy Spirit guiding our path. So, it's not a matter of God being dependent on the angel vs. devil on our shoulders, but God using His Spirit within us to examine our path, our motives, and our direction.

Interpretation #2:

This is what I like to call a literary Yoda-ism. Just as the elder Jedi said to Luke, "Do or do not. There is no try." We have to look closely at the order in which the **King James** translators placed the words. In this instance, I believe the subject is on the opposite side of the verb. My interpretation using the same wording as the 1611 translators would be this:

"The candle of the Lord is searching all the inward parts of the belly – the spirit of man."

The **NLT** takes it a step further and uses the meanings of the Hebrew text to give us this translation:

"27 The Lord's light penetrates the human spirit, exposing every hidden motive."

My takeaway: Regardless of which interpretation you choose, or if you have one of your own, it still is a biblical truth that God knows my inner being intimately and knows my motives for everything I do. I need to listen to His voice and accept His guidance as I travel the path He has chosen for me.

Proverbs 21

The whole premise behind Solomon recording his proverbs was to pass along knowledge to his son. It emphasizes not just the importance but the very NEED for God's chosen to seek wisdom and understanding found in His Word. It also has some very specifically described character traits. Today, while reading this chapter, I came to rest on verse 26. Like so many of the proverbs we find in this book, it paints a stark, contrasting portrait highlighting the difference between the unrighteous and the righteous, the ungodly and the godly. In the **King James Version**, we read:

"26 He coveteth greedily all the day long: but the righteous giveth and spareth not."

Here, we have a very interesting combination of words in the Hebrew text that, at first glance, may seem a bit redundant.

"Coveteth" אָוָה (aw-vaw") means desire…. "greedily" תַאֲוָה (tah-av-aw'} means desire. Perhaps Solomon stuttered? No, what we have is a verb and a noun. The first word, a verb, an action word that speaks of a desire or a craving that supersedes all other thoughts. The second word, while translated as "desire," speaks about the specific object, person, or thought that one craves so intensely. I often think about Esau, who gave away his birthright because he had such an intense hunger, so he traded it for some of Jacob's lentil soup. Sadly, it is often the description of a longing that is never fulfilled, a thirst that is never quenched. Ask most wealthy people if they have enough money, and they'll tell you no amount is enough. The quest continues for more.

The first half of this verse describes the ungodly. The second half is our goal, and I think the **NLT** says it beautifully:

"*²⁶ Some people are always greedy for more, but the godly love to give."*

Several translations use the words, "*but the righteous give and do not hold back.*" This is the very foundation, in my opinion, of the inspired text from Paul given to the Corinthians when he wrote, "*For God loves a cheerful giver*" (II Cor. 9:7).

It inspires me to keep my eyes and ears open as God brings people in need across my path. Yes, I am required to be a good steward of what God has given me, but if there is someone in need and I have the means to be a conduit of God's blessing, then I should not hold back!

My takeaway: First of all, count my blessings. God has been very gracious to me. Secondly, He hasn't blessed me to keep it all to myself but has instructed me to give. Give cheerfully. Give generously. Give intelligently. And give so that God gets the glory and not me.

Proverbs 22

I was excited to share today's passage. As is often the case, no matter how many times I have read through the Proverbs, I always discover a verse that has previously escaped my attention. I'm focusing on verse 18 today, and there's no need to dig into the Hebrew, because the lesson is explicitly clear. Instead, let's look at some translations starting with the **KJV**:

"^{18} *For it is a pleasant thing if thou keep them within thee; they shall withal be fitted in thy lips."*

Our first priority as we read this is to understand what Solomon is referring to as "them" in this passage. We have to backtrack to verse 17 to know he means "the words of the wise."

If ever there was a verse that emphasizes the importance and value of Scripture memorization, Proverbs 22:18 is that verse. Let's look at an even clearer translation from the **NLT**:

"^{18} *For it is good to keep these sayings in your heart and always ready on your lips."*

When Jesus was tempted in the wilderness, He used Scripture to combat the devil. When we read the description of the "whole armor of God" as described by Paul in Ephesians 6:10-18, all the armor is defensive equipment with one exception. The one offensive piece of gear is the sword of the Spirit, which is the Word of God.

I love the **Amplified Version**:

> *"¹⁸ For it will be pleasant if you keep them in mind [incorporating them as guiding principles]; Let them be ready on your lips [to guide and strengthen yourself and others]."*

Bible verse memorization isn't something only for children in Sunday School. All of God's children should be immersed in and intimately familiar with His written word. Make it a habit to commit verses to memory. Every Christian should be able to quote John 3:16 at the drop of a hat, but can you recite other verses to help encourage yourself and others? Can you quote verses to repel the attacks of Satan and his forces? Can you offer comfort using a memorized Scripture verse?

My takeaway: I need to spend more of my time every week learning to take God's love letter, the Bible, and commit as much of it to memory as I can. This is my sword, my weapon to fight temptation, and to be used to strengthen my Christian walk and help me mature in my love and devotion to the One True Holy God of all creation.

Proverbs 23

We have another fantastic lesson to learn from today's verse. This is one of those instances where the passage is pointing to one thing in particular, but the lesson learned can be applied to so much more. In this case, Solomon is describing the dangers of being a drunkard. In verse 35, we read this in the **KJV**:

"^{35} *They have stricken me, shalt thou say, and I was not sick; they have beaten me, and I felt it not: when shall I awake? I will seek it yet again."*

This paints such an accurate picture of someone who is controlled by drunkenness. When "liquored up," you have this idea that you are clever, charming, and completely invincible. I hate to be the bearer of bad news, but booze does not give you Superman's power of invulnerability. I love how the **NLT** describes this verse:

"^{35} *And you will say, "They hit me, but I didn't feel it. I didn't even know it when they beat me up. When will I wake up so I can look for another drink?"*

The utterly ridiculous thing is the response of the befuddled sot once he regains consciousness. "Holy cow! When did I get beat up? I don't even remember it! I think I'll go get another drink!"

It's true that alcohol abuse can destroy practically anything it touches, but as I mentioned earlier, I believe this text can apply to any sin in the book, from the illegal use of drugs to spousal abuse to petty theft to porn addiction and so much more. Satan whispers in our ear, "Try it, you'll like it!"

There's this very temporary moment of delight and satisfaction, and in the midst of sin, we are valiant beasts tamed by no one. But once we wake up, we wonder, "What happened?" "How did I get into this predicament?" We have that brief moment of self-loathing, then decide to "look for another drink (or fill in your preferred vice)" so we can feel super again.

My takeaway: I need to cry out to the Holy God of the Universe to fill me with His Spirit and allow Him to give me the strength needed to turn away from any sinful desire – *"the lust of the flesh, the lust of the eyes, and the pride of life"*. (I John 2:16) I need to understand that temporary satisfaction is a horrible excuse for an eternity of regret.

Proverbs 24

One of the precepts that has long been fascinating to me and one that I have tried to strengthen in my life is faith. While seeing is believing, faith is believing without seeing. It's a building block of Christianity. Jesus Himself even said, *"Blessed are those who have not seen and have believed."* That being said, I think it is extremely important that we don't dismiss the fine art of seeing. This was really drilled home for me today as I read the 24th chapter of Proverbs. Once again, we have a chapter rich with multiple "sayings" of the king to his son. When we get to verses 30-34, it becomes less of a saying and more about a narrative. In the story, Solomon says he walked past the field of a "sluggard" (a lazy person) and noticed the field was overgrown with weeds and thorns. Even the stone wall built to contain the field was broken down to rubble from a lack of care and maintenance. Verse 32 of the **NIV** says:

"³² I applied my heart to what I observed
and learned a lesson from what I saw."

Pop the clutch of your brain and back up to chapter 20, where we read in verse 12 that eyes to see are a gift from God. Yes, faith is believing without seeing, but God gave us eyes to also see to reinforce our faith and beliefs.

"Applied to my heart" – this is taken from two separate Hebrew words. The first, שִׁית (sheeth), means to put, consider, to fix it in place. Think about laying a piece of ceramic tile on the floor. You don't just plop it down. You apply an adhesive and fix it in place. Once applied and given time to set, it doesn't move.

The second word, לֵב (labe) refers to the inner man, your mind, your heart. The observed scene of the ruination of this field because of a slothful, lazy person isn't just one of those "would you look at that" moments, only to be forgotten. This image of failed farming and the reason why was "set in place" on his heart, his mind, his understanding so that it would serve as a valuable lesson for all of life. *"A little sleep, a little slumber, a little folding of the hands to rest – and poverty will come on you like a thief and scarcity like an armed man."* (vv. 33-34)

But what really stood out to me in this passage (referring back to verse 32), is the whole "learned a lesson" statement. This isn't an "A-ha" moment. The word translated as "lesson" is from the Hebrew מוּסָר (moo-sawr'), and it means to be given chastisement, reproof, or discipline. It tells me that I, just like Solomon, used the eyes God gave me and pointed out the ruin that slothfulness can generate and reminds me of the times I have been lazy and unwilling to work for my Lord. It disciplines me with the thought that, but for the grace of the Almighty, I would be in the same place of ruin.

My takeaway: I must always be at the point that I am *"pressing (working) toward the mark for the prize of the high calling of God in Christ Jesus."* Philippians 3:14

Proverbs 25

Today, we will look at a verse that has had several different interpretations over the years. To me, I don't really understand the confusion, but let's take a look at it together. This is also a good time to emphasize that one of the purposes of this devotional is to encourage the reader to do their own research and study.

Today, we are looking at Proverbs 25:11. Let's start with the **KJV**:

> *"11 A word fitly spoken is like apples of gold in pictures of silver."*

My paternal grandmother had a small devotional book that I remember seeing called Apples of Gold. It came with its own bookmark: a gold-colored metallic clip with an apple on the top. This has nothing to do with the devotional, but it's a memory that always surfaces when I read this verse.

What I find very interesting here is that the word אֹפֶן (o-fawn') that is translated as "fitly" occurs over 30 times in the Old Testament, and this is the ONLY time it was translated as "fitly." Every other place it is used, the translation is "wheel." The very root word in Hebrew means to revolve. A literal translation would be "a word wheel." To me (again, just my opinion. Research it for yourself to prove me right or wrong!), this refers to words or advice given at the right place, at the right time. It's a theological "what goes around comes around" concept. One of the reasons I believe this is because of another of King Solomon's writings in the book of Ecclesiastes.

In the third chapter, we read, "*For everything there is a season, and a time for every matter under heaven.*"

The apples of gold in "pictures" of silver is better translated as gold apples set against a carved setting of silver. The actual root meaning of this word is a bit of a mystery, but if you take the two most precious metals of the day, gold and silver, and create a carved figure of gold apples against a silver backdrop, the stark difference between the two colors and the shimmer of the metal would create a beautiful, valuable, and most-prized possession. I think, perhaps, this could have been a very piece of art owned by Solomon and how he marveled at its beauty every time he looked at it.

That beauty, that wonder, that appreciation of art is the same response when you either give or receive a word given at the right time, right place. Given my hypothetical circumstance of King Solomon's artwork, I tend to prefer verse 11 as read in the **NLT**:

"*[11] Timely advice is lovely, like golden apples in a silver basket.*"

My takeaway: As I have often read in Proverbs to exercise wisdom by keeping my mouth shut, I must also be ready to offer a kind word, some requested advice, or loving reproach. I believe I can know when the right time is to give the right word by always seeking and asking my heavenly Father for wisdom and understanding.

Proverbs 26

Our devotional today takes a different course. As I was reading Proverbs 26, I ran across two successive verses that, by all appearances, seem to completely contradict each other. I once heard someone say if there is a single error in the Bible, then it is all a lie.

Well, I, for one, cannot believe there is such a blatant "Uh-Oh" as what we will look at today. Read the verses from the **NLT**, and you tell me. Is this a contradiction?

> "*4 Don't answer the foolish arguments of fools,*
> *or you will become as foolish as they are.*
> *5 Be sure to answer the foolish arguments of fools,*
> *or they will become wise in their own estimation.*"

My first thought was the translators obviously made a mistake here. These are two separately worded phrases in the Hebrew text………. Nope. I looked it up. It's the very same wording used. Instead of throwing my hands up in exasperation, it's time to step back and look at this from both an historical and a literary point of view.

It was a very common practice in Hebrew poetry to use parallelism. We see it throughout the Old Testament. What that means is the writers would use verbal constructs with grammatical similarities. While the two parallel thoughts were related, they also had a slightly different meaning. A great example of parallelism is the phrase, "Easy come. Easy go."

Verse 4 is a warning that it is pointless to argue with a fool on his own terms. In other words, using deception, sarcasm, ridicule, etc. Basically, it lowers you to his level. This is typically where you just need to ignore them, or as written, *"don't answer."*

Verse 5, on the other hand, lets us know that there will be times when you need to answer, but while the fool is arguing, your response should be reproof or correction. A good example is given to us by Solomon's father, King David, in Psalm 14:1 when he wrote, *"The fool hath said in his heart, 'There is no God.'"* In these cases, you do want to answer or reprove *"or they will become wise in their own estimation."*

Passages like these are the very reason we should, as the Proverbs pointed out in the very beginning, be diligent and actively seek and ask for wisdom, knowledge, and understanding. When the unlearned fools or the deceitful and deliberate wicked throw apparent contradictions of God's Word in our faces, we need to have the knowledge to answer and defend the faith.

My takeaway: Studying God's Word was never promised to be easy, but it is a necessity as a Christian to know what I believe, why I believe it, and how to defend it.

Proverbs 27

Today I would like to offer an example of why it's not always the best thing to rely solely upon the King's English as written in the mid-17th century. Our passage in Proverbs 27 is verse 12a as read in the **KJV**:

"12 A prudent man foreseeth the evil, and hideth himself."

Let's begin with who this prudent man is. The Hebrew word is עָרוּם (aw-room'), and it means to be crafty, sensible, and shrewd. Quite often, it is a description used in a negative sense, but here, we see it in a positive light because of the outcome of "foreseeing" evil and "hiding" from it. Other instances of this word in a positive light can be found in the following verses in Proverbs, each describing the result of being a prudent man:

12:16 – overlooks an insult

12:23 – keeps his knowledge

14:8 – gives thought to their ways

14:15 – gives thought to his steps

14:18 – crowned with knowledge

22:3 – sees danger and takes refuge

The overall characteristic of being prudent is someone who – with knowledge, wisdom, and understanding provided by the Lord – has common sense and knows how and when to use it.

The word translated as a simple foreseeth, רָאָה (raw-aw'), does have the simple translation "to see." However, this same word is used more than any other word in the Old Testament when describing the "seeing" or receiving of a vision, oracle, prophesy of an authentic prophet from God. It is a truth that cannot be questioned. The word also conveys the meaning of advising yourself or to inspect.

Now we know who and what. A man or woman with knowledge, understanding, and a cranium full of common sense can thoroughly and capably inspect a situation or a worldly viewpoint and come to a logical conclusion. The next step is to determine what to do with that knowledge.

According to the **KJV**, we are to hide ourselves. Ok, all you stubborn KJ-Vites…here's where your God-given common sense needs to step to the forefront. Is God really asking you to hide? *"Finally, my brethren, put on the whole armor of God, that ye may be able to [hide from] the devil…"* No.

If I'm to hide, then why do I need armor? Our armor has a sword. A sword is for fighting, not hiding. "Resist the devil, and he will flee from you." God NEVER said to hide from the devil. Who lights a candle and hides it under a bushel? No, let your light so shine before men.

This word, סָתַר (saw-thar'), conveys the idea of concealing, secret. It's a quiet preparation that you keep close. Yes, it can mean to hide. It's the same word that describes how David hid from Saul. But in our passage, when put in the setting of a person using their common sense to see something amiss, our duty is to quietly prepare… Check to see that all our armor is in place before stepping in front of the roaring lion walking about seeking whom he may devour.

No, we don't run TOWARD evil, but neither do we run FROM it. We stand. We fight. But only AFTER we prepare. Think of these Bible-related instances about those who listened and prepared:

Noah – He didn't wait for the rain to start and hope for God to miraculously send a Royal Caribbean cruise ship. He prepared, even in the midst of ridicule. He didn't hide. He built.

When **Jesus** Himself said in Matthew 6 not to worry about tomorrow, His command was not to WORRY. In his letter to the church at Philippi, the apostle **Paul** wrote to be anxious for nothing. Once again, this speaks of worrying. Anxiety has no place in the Christian walk, but using your mind and common sense, seeing an oncoming concern and preparing to meet it… Well, that's Biblical, my friends.

My takeaway: There is nothing questionable nor sinful about being prepared for the future. The wrongdoing comes when there is fear, anxiety, and/or worry attached to the actions of my preparations. My trust comes from the Lord, but so does my common sense.

Proverbs 28

Let's take our daily verse and make it a companion to what we learned yesterday. In verse 1, we have a comparison between the wicked and the godly. Almost all translations agree on the wording. Let's look at the **NIV**:

> *"¹ The wicked flee though no one pursues, but the righteous are as bold as a lion."*

We aren't going to concern ourselves with the wicked today, but the latter half of the verse confirms our argument from yesterday when it says the righteous are as bold as lions. There's really no deep, hidden meaning tucked away inside of these words. This is a plainly spoken truth as is. But, just for grins and giggles, let's see what is meant by describing the righteous or godly as bold.

The Hebrew word used is בָּטַח (baw-takh'). It's one of two words that can be translated as bold, but this particular word also carries the idea of confidence and being secure. Unlike its counterpart, though, this word stresses that the confidence that is exuded comes only from having something or someone in whom that confidence is placed.

If we combine yesterday's devotional with today's, our lesson is clear: Using our common sense to detect the approach of evil, we prepare to meet it. We put on the whole armor of God, draw our Sword of the Spirit and stand, knowing our confidence that makes us bold as a lion comes directly from the Lion of Judah.

A translation I rarely use is **The Voice Bible**. I don't particularly recommend this when it comes to Bible study. It's a translation that employs not only scholars of language, but it "jazzes up" the Word by also using artists like poets and musicians to add to the presentation. As a result, I think it can be questionable with its accuracy. Nonetheless, there are times when the aforementioned presentation is worth reading. The way the **VOICE** puts it:

> "*[1] The right-living, however, stand their ground as boldly as lions.*"

I like that. We stand our ground. Unmovable. Fierce. Ready to not just fight but to conquer.

My takeaway: I definitely treasure my peace and tranquility, but there are wicked, unrighteous powers and principalities in the world. The fact of the matter is that if I am to do my duty as a child of God, then not only WILL there be a fight, but I must be prepared to stand my ground and face the enemy with the boldness provided solely in my trust in God and His Son, Jesus.

Proverbs 29

Proverbs was written to be an instruction manual for the Christian walk. It is a book full of many repeating "How-To's" along with a road map that not only shows us the proper way to travel, but also points out the paths along the way to avoid. As we delve into this chapter, we will learn the differences and definitions of pride, humiliation, humility, and honor. Let's read verse 23 from the **NLT**:

"²³ Pride ends in humiliation, while humility brings honor."

In this one small verse, we see two distinct and very opposing paths. The first path is called Pride. It is often confusing, because there are most definitely portions of my life where I happily and unashamedly exhibit pride. I am extremely proud of my daughter and my grandkids. I take pride in the work I do. Does this verse warn me that my final destination is humiliation because of this pride? Not at all.

The word used for pride is גַּאֲוָה (gah-av-aw'), and it describes arrogance and haughtiness. It is used in the Old Testament extensively as a negative trait referencing a lifestyle that lives in the realm of condemnation.

However, we do occasionally see traits that we view as 100% negative in a positive light. Anger is a good example. Is anger 100% wrong? If so, why did the Apostle Paul instruct the church at Ephesus to *"be angry and sin not"*? (Eph.4:26) This type of anger is often referred to as "righteous wrath." No matter how you label it, the fact remains that it is still anger, and it is positively endorsed by the Spirit-inspired Word.

I believe, like anger, some of our pride is acceptable and endorsed. However, THIS pride of verse 23 has a path that leads nowhere but to the doorstep of humiliation. The word used is שָׁפֵל (shaw-fale') which means to be abased, brought low. The visual is to be INVOLUNTARILY brought to your knees. Quite the opposite picture of what was intended when pumping yourself up with the hot air of pride in the hopes of rising above everyone else in a show of arrogant superiority.

The second path is called Humility. Oddly enough, it is from the exact same root word that we had above that is translated as humiliation. This variation, however, שָׁפָל (shaw-fawl') also describes the position of baseness with one exception. Instead of being FORCED to one's knees, the person WILLINGLY stoops low. To me, it paints a beautiful portrait of a prayer warrior.

The "X Marks the Spot" of this path is honor. The Hebrew is כָּבוֹד (kaw-bode'). It describes a position of splendor and glory. It can be a literal place of honor, but often describes a character trait or reputation seen and respected by others. This is the path we should be following.

My takeaway: Pompous arrogance may start out by inflating my ego, but I better realize that kind of self-centered gassiness will eventually pop my reality balloon. My path is to always be willing to kneel down in prayer and seek God's guidance in my life. I need to always seek His lamp, lighting the path of humility and follow in His steps.

Proverbs 30

We see an odd happenstance with this chapter as the author is identified as Agur, the son of Jakeh. Does that mean we are no longer reading the proverbs of Solomon? Possibly. Possibly not. There is a debate among scholars as to whether or not Agur is a real person. Some suggest he is a literary creation of Solomon. Personally, I have no reason to doubt Agur's existence. The chapter identifies him, his father Jakeh, and the students he is speaking to who probably were writing these proverbs down as he spoke them. Either way, I view this chapter as part of God's inspired Word. I was particularly drawn to verses 24-28, which tells us of four things that are little but wise. Here are the verses as read in the **KJV**:

> "*24 There be four things which are little upon the earth, but they are exceeding wise:*
>
> *25 The ants are a people not strong, yet they prepare their meat in the summer;*
>
> *26 The conies are but a feeble folk, yet make they their houses in the rocks;*
>
> *27 The locusts have no king, yet go they forth all of them by bands;*
>
> *28 The spider taketh hold with her hands, and is in kings' palaces.*"

We could spend considerable time researching and speculating on the different animals mentioned, but that really isn't the point being made. However, to clear up any confusion, my studies have confirmed the animals are the ant, the rock badger, the locust, and the spider. The two that seem to give most people issues are the rock badger and the spider.

The word "conies" is just another name for the rock badger, sometimes called a hyrax or rock rabbit. It's a little rodent-looking mammal native to Africa and the Middle East. The title "badger" would make you think they are pretty fierce. The truth, however, is they are fairly low on the food chain, and almost anything that breathes would consider them a good bite to eat. Weak as they are, though, they know how to use the rocks as both their home and their protection. Pretty smart for a Scooby snack.

The spider, I've noticed, is translated as "lizard" in several translations. I'm on Team Arachnid, because I feel the portrait being painted focuses on what the animal does with "her hands." Think of a tiny little spider and the magnificent creations she can make with her webs. Other translations want to focus on the animal being easily caught with the hand. For some reason, it seems more probable that people would more readily catch a lizard with their hands than they would a spider. But here's the thing: If you want to join Team Reptile, it doesn't lessen the value of the verse. It's OK to be a spider or a lizard.

My takeaway: In the world's eyes, I may be insignificant (ant), but I can be industrious. I may be weak (rock badger), but I have wisdom from God. I may be small (locust), but I am in unity with Christ and His chosen. I may be reviled (spider), but I can still create beauty and wonder through my dependence on the Holy God of all creation.

Proverbs 31

As we put a bow on the month of Proverbs, we finish out with a very specific instruction when it comes to those who are not able to have a voice and will often face great injustice. Let's look at verse 8 in the **NIV**:

> "*⁸ Speak up for those who cannot speak for themselves, for the rights of all who are destitute.*"

Let's be clear. This is not an endorsement for vigilantism. In no way does this suggest that I should put on red tights and a cape. I don't want that. Trust me, you don't want to see that. So, let's break down the words used.

First, those who cannot speak for themselves do not refer to a group with a physical ailment. The word used, אִלֵּם (il-lame') conveys the idea of muteness or silence that has been forced, whether legally or physically. These are people who don't have the means to defend themselves in a verbal argument. Our concept of being "tongue-tied" is derived from this word.

What are the rights we are to defend? Translated as "cause" in the **KJV**, this word דִּין (doon) refers to imposed justice or a sentence. To me, it can describe an unjust penalty or even unfair treatment, especially by those who would abuse their power or authority.

Don't be fooled when reading the second half of this verse. "*All those who are destitute*" is not a broadly painted, secondary character trait of "*those who cannot speak for themselves.*" It can

INCLUDE them, but there's more than meets the eye here. This is, in actuality, a different description. In the **King James Version**, it reads, "appointed בֵּן (bane) to destruction" חָלוֹף (khal-ofe')." The literal translations would be describing a family entity, usually a son or grandson. It speaks of a vanishing, to abolish. In some cases, it can refer to being orphaned. Isn't it interesting that later in the New Testament times, the Apostle Paul clearly points out orphans as a group the church should take responsibility for in caring and providing their needs?

My takeaway: Whether due to bigotry, hatred, prejudice, or even an unjust law, my duty is to stand up for and defend those who have been forced into silence or are facing unrighteous penalties for nothing more than being who they are. Additionally, it is not the government, but the church…. narrow it in….ME….who should be caring for orphans. Time, talent, finances…. Anything I may devote to this is part of my obedience and tithing to the work of the Kingdom.

Conclusion

As I stated at the beginning of this devotional, my sincere desire is that you will have your own 2-part takeaway from reading this book.

First, I pray that the insight and blessings that have been graciously given to me through God's Holy Spirit will find their way into your hearts and minds so that you may also experience those blessings.

Second, it is my hope that you will be inspired and motivated to create your own 31 Days of Proverbs, whereby you will receive your own blessings from above and then to share those blessings with all those around you.

From there, expand your horizon and become a student of the Word. Study the Psalms. Live a vicarious life of Jesus by digging into all four Gospels. Choose a book of the Bible that, perhaps, you have never read in full. Books like Job, Ezra, and Esther. The Minor Prophets. Cultivate a craving for the daily bread, the manna, the Scriptures.

Begin every day with a time of quiet devotion spent in prayer, worship, and reading the Bible. Ask every day for wisdom, knowledge, and understanding. Keep a daily journal of what you've read and what you learned.

As the Apostle Peter wrote, *"Grow in the grace and knowledge of our Lord and Savior Jesus Christ. To him be glory both now and forever! Amen."*